Indian Legends of the White Mountains

Indian Legends of the White Mountains

by J. S. English

Table of Contents

Chocorua

The White Mountains have well deserved the title now so generally bestowed upon them—"The Marvelous Crystal Hills." Caverns, precipitous cliffs and ravines, appalling, yet attractive in their awful grandeur, and the pastoral vision of fresh mountain brooks and verdant valleys, trickling cascades, waterfalls and imposing yet alluring mountain peaks, have thrilled with interest the visitor to a region where nature masses so many wonders.

Superbly grand and gorgeous is the vista; and he who is acquainted with the hallowed memories which repose in these lofty peaks, the tales which have sprung from those cavern depths, or the primitive associations of the silvery cascades and waterfalls, woven together in the sacred legends and lore of a savage nation, will say that his vision is broader and his perception plainer. As the sunlight unfolds to the eye a view of charms, rare in their magnificence — so in the dark and hidden recesses, where the eye must hesitate, the mind's vision lays bare the secrets of the long ago, pictured in the sunlight setting of the present.

Barren and bleak, rugged and forbidding, the peak of Chocorua looms like a temple tower or a fortress, such as giants in ancient times used in their wars against the gods. Utterly devoid of vegetation, the gray summit flanked by the other domes of the Sandwich Range which lie around, it speaks plainly of a day centuries gone, when the tales of the Red Sokokis were born within its rocky breast.

Chocorua, although 3540 feet in height, grows nothing but Alpine vegetation, and the bald, sharp summit has a narrow ridge much lower than the summit running to the northeast. Deep ravines and defiles mark the mountain side. It is very accessible, being approached by carriage, foot and bridle paths to a spur upon which a shelter house has been built; but the last stage of the journey to the summit must be made on foot, as the remainder of the route is entirely over steep ledges. From the summit, like a pinnacle tower, one can look over the entire wilderness. Chocorua has not changed — thus she appeared when first the white man entered her forest.

At the advent of the early settlers, the Sokokis, a numerous and powerful Indian tribe, were in possession of the country now comprising Northern New Hampshire and the Maine borderland. Chocorua, who lived in the neighborhood of the mountain, was chief of a mighty tribe. He had watched the white man's ingress and had battled for the land of his fathers; but, as the settlers advanced, he retreated into the wild fastnesses of the forest, among the mountains, and here with the remnants of his tribe he lived for a time unharassed and unhampered by the pale-face. Tall and shapely, like the chiefs of his race, but more powerful than the others, he roamed the forests, a monarch. He hunted the deer and the moose, furnished his tepee with the skins of the bear, trapped the beaver and the mink and speared the salmon. Powerful in the councils of his nation, he was a warrior of renown. Already he had faced the white man's powder and his scalp locks were many. He had seen his land encroached upon, his supply of game and food wantonly destroyed and the "Black Robe" had entered to dispel his hopes of a Great Spirit, a Gitche Manitou, who would protect the red man in his wars and guide him in the chase. The heart of Chocorua was big, and at the council fires he spoke to the young braves, infused them with tales of his prowess and the record of their tribe, and bade them listen only to the voice of the Manitou and heed the advice of the wise men. They had been driven back by the white settlers, while the Great Spirit slept, but when Manitou awoke from his slumbers and spoke in his voice of thunder from the peak of the mountain, he would direct the Indians how to drive the invaders from their lands.

Chocorua had a son, a young boy of twelve who gamboled and frolicked with the papooses, but as lithe and agile as a fawn. Sturdy in limb, a robust little fellow, dexterous in his use of the bow and arrow, oftentimes he followed his father in the chase, climbing the cliffs in search of eagles' eggs, bounding over rocky ledges, scrambling up the mountain sides in pursuit of the moose or paddling his bark canoe over the still waters of the lake. Ever watchful of this young "lion, " untamed and savage, careless as the panther which leaped from limb to limb, Chocorua looked with loving eyes on the stalwart shape of his young son. He pictured the time when the sinews in those arms would stand out like his own; when that hearing already acute would rival that of the animals which he hunted; when the features which now relaxed and smiled would become as strong and impassive as his own brown countenance; when the scalp axe would dangle at his belt and, decorated in the glories of his war paint, the son of Chocorua would go forth a brave. Ah, then! then would the voice of the Great Spirit in tones of thunder direct the red man, and again would the Sokokis be the most powerful among the nations.

Every day Chocorua would journey to the mountain top to beseech the Manitou, and from this tower he would scan the horizon. Great was his surprise one day to see beyond the tepees of his tribe, curls of blue smoke arising. Gazing intently, his keen eyes observed that the volume of smoke came not from the wigwam of an Indian but from the fire of a pale-face. Long and earnestly did Chocorua watch the wreaths of blue smoke as they ascended to the clouds. The white man had again invaded his domains. Chocorua was sad.

Settlers had surely come; ere long a few cabins were erected and the white invaders industriously commenced to till the ground and cultivate the fields. Fearful of the white man's power, yet distrustful of his purpose, the Indians were by no means friendly, yet, through fear, they were held in abeyance. Chocorua showed no sign of enmity, rather he seemed to cultivate the friendship of the pale-faces, for he gave them of his corn, bartered with pelts and skins for their goods, and in other ways was amicably disposed. His little son had learned to like the ways of the "white squaw" and in the white man's wigwam many a sweet bit he received from the good housewife. Almost every day he called but he was neglecting none the less his savage lessons, for the forest was his playground and the hunt his sport. One day as he visited the house he found on the table a cup which he supposed contained coffee and of which he had become very fond. He raised it to his lips and drank the contents. Instantly he became ill, and the good woman hurrying to the scene discovered the cause—the cup had contained poison.

He was tenderly removed to the wigwam of Chocorua. The medicine men were called and their potions and charms administered, but to no avail. With the stoical demeanor of his race, the boy related the cause of his trouble and with face utterly inexpressive of pain or emotion he answered willingly as he had been taught, the message of the Great Spirit. Chocorua strode from his wigwam his countenance unchanged; but in his heart was the culmination of a long frustrated desire—revenge! death! The white man had followed him. He had plucked from his bosom the fire of his life, the hope of his race; he had murdered his father, his brothers and his child. The Manitou had spoken. He could hear his voice in the winds. The time had come; the accursed pale-faces must die and their scalps would dangle at his belt. First he must appease the Great Spirit and satisfy the cravings of his heart—revenge for his son. Silently wending his way through the forests to the cabin of the settler, Chocorua halted in the distance and then patiently waited for the departure of the husband. Yes, he must kill first the baby and the mother; and then after the husband had viewed their scalpless bodies, his scalp, too, would follow. At length the husband departed. Furtively watching and waiting, Chocorua crept toward the door and then with a bound and an exultant war whoop the tomahawk descended—mother and child lay lifeless. The father returned to find the mutilated bodies of his family. He loaded his rifle and departed from the house. He wandered to the wigwam of Chocorua; the chief was absent. All night he waited in ambush, but no return. In the morning he journeyed up the mountain, and when near the summit the white man and the chief of the Sokokis met face to face. The muzzle of the white man's rifle met the Indian's breast. Backward, step by step, Chocorua was forced until he reached the summit; then standing on the edge of the precipice, the Indian with eyes aflame and in a voice of wrath said, "Chocorua will go no further! He bids the white man defiance! Chocorua will go to the Great Spirit with the scalps of the white man's squaw and his papoose! He will hunt and shoot and fish in the Happy Hunting Grounds with his son and his fathers!" Then his eyes flashed in a look of defiance, the pent-up hatred of his heart shone in his bronze features, his chest rose and heaved, and raising his hand he spoke thus: "Chocorua curses the pale-face and his children; his curse and the curse of his Manitou on the white man's cattle! May the drought come on his crops! May the earth bum under him and may the red man's revenge follow him forever! Chocorua will die, but not by the white man's cannon!" and the warrior chief turned and sprang from the precipice into the frightful abyss below.

The white settler left the vicinity and wandered no one knows where. The Indians for a long time were unmolested, but pestilence and warfare gradually depopulated the Sokokis. They no longer remained the powerful and war-like tribe of former years. Eventually, white settlers came to Albany at the foot of Chocorua Mountain, but the land was unsuited for crops, and the cattle who grazed in the vicinity and drank from the water died in a short while. The land where the white man and the Indian met is a barren spot, while the soil and forest about the peak years since were devastated by fire; and the mountain cranberries, dwarfed blueberries and Alpine vegetation which flourish in the crevices of the rock, are the only flora to be found on the summit. Scientists say that the lime formation from the rocks has poisoned the soil; but tradition says the curse of Chocorua remains on the region.

Sacred to the Indians was the vicinity of Chocorua after the death of the chief, and Chocorua Lake was looked upon as the Manitou's blessed water. And woe be unto him, whose voice was heard over its waters, for the wrath of the Great Spirit was such that instantly the offender and his canoe would sink to the bottom of the lake.

Mount Washington

Lofty, cloud-piercing "Agiochook!" How thy enshrouded summit impressed the simple superstitious mind of the imaginative Indian! How his fanatical soul, filled with the religious zeal of the red savage, shrank in terror from thy angry moods and gazed fondly and reverently in admiration at thy kinder countenance.

To the Indians "Agiochook," which meant "The place of the Great Spirit of the forest," was a mysterious world, a land reaching to their heaven, which the Manitou visited and enriched with his presence. "Agiochook" was a general term applied to all the territory encompassed by the White Mountains, but more particularly to Mt. Washington. Monarch among the mountains, the loftiest peak, Mt. Washington, was a fitting place for the Manitou, from which to deal forth his desires, whether punishment or reward.

This region was populated principally by the Abenakis, the Sokokis or Pequawkets and the Pemigewassets. These Indians were advanced over their neighbors in many of the customs of civilization and today, in mounds in the vicinity, are found traces of their former habitation—rough earthenware dishes, tomahawks of an improved style, and various utensils showing an advance ahead of the average New England tribes. Their superstitions were many, and their legends which had been handed down from generation to generation were sacredly believed in and adhered to.

Regarding Mt. Washington, it was their belief that countless ages back the entire world except the White Mountains was destroyed. The great Manitou had been displeased at his children and in his wrath sent a dreadful deluge, which completely submerged the earth. A great powwow and his wife fled to the mountains and by the aid of the Manitou were lifted to the summit of Mt. Washington. They brought with them a hare, and after the deluge had ceased and they had been on the mountain top for many moons, the powwow released the hare. It scampered down the mountain side, but after a time returned carrying some dry blades of grass in his mouth. They then

13

descended the mountain and finding the flood had subsided, they built a tepee. They lived here for a number of years and had many children, and from them sprang the Abenaki Indians.

The Giant's Grave

At Fabyan, New Hampshire, near the foot of Mt. Washington and close by the side of the present Fabyan House, was a mound about thirty feet in height known as the Giant's Grave, the burial tomb of some prehistoric sagamore, who had successfully led his followers in battle against the other nation. Great was his prowess and marvelous his strength, and when at last he felt the breath of life departing, he selected this mound as his tomb. Standing on the hill which should be his grave, on a dark night, he waved a burning firebrand o'er his head, and in a voice which echoed to the mountain tops cried:

"No pale-face shall take deep root here; This the Great Spirit whispered in my ear."

Notwithstanding the prophecy of the sagamore, Ethan Allen Crawford, the mountain pioneer, built a hotel in 1803, but it was destroyed by fire sixteen years later. Two other hotels were afterward erected, but the giant's torch alike fell upon them and they too were burned. Not until the mound was razed and the present Fabyan House erected was the curse dispelled.

Tradition tells the legend of the giant's curse. History relates the fact of the burning of the hotels. It is for the reader to determine which has priority.

Nancy's Brook

Where is the person who has visited the White Hills, gazed upon the splendor of the lofty peaks and the acres of green- backed forest; upon the rushing, roaring waterfalls which leap and thunder over huge precipices; upon the trickling mountain rivulets and silvery cascades, and the hundred and one curiosities fashioned by the hand of Nature among her favored hills, who does not carry away with him the tale of the wild? The craggy cliff whose forbidding front defies the mountain climber, whose topmost point bends forward over a bottomless chasm, or the deep, rugged ravine whose jaws open like some mammoth monster, leading into regions of darkness and mystery—these are the mirrors of bloody tales, reflecting the tragic events of the legendary past and the historical horrors of another generation. But in the quiet green vales and the flowing forest fields, a different picture is portrayed — gayous and happy in their mirthful dance, the waving grass and the gorgeous flowers betoken memoirs of an age when Indian lovers fondly strolled listening to the songs of the birds and the music of the forest; and when the dashing young brave in the exuberance of his youth zealously followed in the chase. Again, on the borders of the forest, the vision of happiness lingers lovingly, only to change in the sonorous recesses of the wood, with the doleful sighing of the pines. The silvery waters of the mountain brook have lost their sunshine, and the hurrying cascade murmurs a music in accompaniment to the sobs of the trees.

It is true, "Nature has a voice of gladness and of sorrow," and gazing into the waters of Nancy's Brook, I heard only the mournful notes and read only the tale of sorrow.

Rising among cliffs of forbidding aspect, it courses through rocky clefts, hollowed by centuries of usage; winding around giant boulders, through caverns deep in their descent and perpendicular walls rising as high as thirty feet on both sides. Leaping over mountain heights, sobbing in its downward surge, wild and sorrowful even in its snatches of sunshine, and gloomier yet

17

in its path of shadow, this impressive mountain stream follows through the wood not far from the site of the present Crawford House.

Nancy was a beautiful maiden, a servant in the family of Colonel Whipple, who resided at Jefferson. Colonel Whipple was a prominent man in early affairs of the colony, and had many servants. Nancy had become engaged to one of the men in the Colonel's employ, and preparations had been made for the marriage. They were to journey to Portsmouth where the ceremony was to be performed.

It was a cold winter's day when Nancy, happy and smiling, after receiving her two years' wages from the Colonel and entrusting it to the care of her lover, started for Lancaster to make some necessary purchases requisite for the journey. She spent the day in Lancaster and toward dusk returned to Jefferson. On reaching the Colonel's house she was amazed and startled to find that her betrothed had left previously for Portsmouth. Frenzied and distracted, the poor girl determined to follow in pursuit. In vain the men sought to dissuade her, and wearied from her Lancaster journey she entered the forests toward Portsmouth.

Wild and bleak is a winter among the forests of the White Hills. The wind howled and raged through the branches of the forest; the snow fell thick and fast about her, and rising before her the white- capped hills in unfriendly mien refused their help. No path to steer the weary way of the forlorn traveler; no voice save the cruel tones of the storm and the curdling howls of the wolves. Plodding as best she could this brave woman suffered no hardship to alter her determination—she must reach the Crawford Notch—for here the Colonel had a shelter cabin where he was wont to stop on his journeys to and from Portsmouth. She must reach the cabin before morning, and she felt confident she would find the objects of her search. Floundering in the huge heaps of snow which blocked her passage, numb and freezing from the bitter blasts, she at length reached the hut; but already he had come and gone. Not many hours had elapsed since the departure though, as the embers on the hearth were yet alive. Stopping only long enough to rest her tired limbs, she left the hut, dragging herself through the blinding snow she pressed on; but wearied beyond the power of human endurance, even she, possessed as she was of almost indomitable courage, could go no farther, and on the banks of the icy brook she sat down to rest. With her head bent forward leaning upon her staff, utterly exhausted, she had reached the last stage of her journey.

At Jefferson, the men at first supposed she would return, after recognizing the fruitlessness and difficulties of her errand, but later realizing the perilous position of the girl, they set out in search of her. Piloting through the forests, expecting at every moment to find her dead body buried in the snow, they were surprised to discover traces of her visit to the cabin, but little was their encouragement, for but a short stretch beyond they came to the brook and there, seated on the bank, her head inclined on her staff, frozen in death was the maidservant, Nancy. The roaring of the storm had ceased; the forest, clad in its snow-white shroud, uttered no sound to disturb the sacredness of the dead; only the brook babbled on, mournfully voicing its protest.

The faithless lover not long afterward suffered the deserts of the wicked, he became a maniac and until his death which occurred shortly afterward in a mad house, he pleaded for forgiveness from his faithful Nancy.

When the snow clouds gather now around Nancy's Brook and the wind whistles and howls in discordant tones, from the piercing cold of the snowy hills the shrieks of the madman are heard, and then softer and yet distinctly audible, from the borders of the brook, waft the soft, low, heart-breaking sighs of the deserted girl.

The Red Carbuncle

To enter a land which the Great Spirit had hallowed with his presence! Not for all the treasures of the earth would the red man pass into that forbidden paradise; and woe unto the desecrator who presumed to venture thither.

Once, two great Powwows, who had grown bold because of their success at magic, attempted to ascend the mountain but were never afterward heard from. So perished all who defied the power of the Manitou.

When the storms raged, the shrieks of the evil spirits who were confined in the caverns of the mountains resounded in the valleys below. When angry, the Great Spirit in a voice of thunder proclaimed his rage from the mountain top. Offenders against his laws were struck by flashes of fire from heaven and from his home on the mountain peak he dispensed plague and drought and all ills which befell the red man.

Suspended from a dangerous ledge on the peak of Mt. Washington was a monstrous carbuncle which shone with a dazzling red and golden luster at night. Like the rays of the rising morning sun, this luminous jewel lighted the mountain top for miles around. Fortunate was the being who touched this precious stone, for henceforth it acted as a talisman and no danger could befall him on land or sea. But it was safely guarded by an evil spirit, a wicked Indian who had climbed the mountain top in defiance of the Manitou and who, as a punishment, had been killed, and his spirit stationed as a guard to perpetually watch over the stone. In his hand he held a fiery spear, and the human being who approached was bound to be enveloped in a haze of mist and smoke. The lake below rumbled and roared; then bewildered and frightened at the point of the spear, the intruder was pushed over the precipice into this steaming and boiling lake, and the victim lost forever.

The Indians were not alone in their visions of the Carbuncle for after the white settlers advent it was seen, and a party of white men journeyed to the mountain top in search of it. They claimed that they had located it but owing to the danger of being dashed to pieces in reaching it they returned, being

21

satisfied with large quantities of quartz and crystals, which they gathered supposing them to be diamonds.

Another party was afterward organized, but after a hazardous trip, during which they experienced all sorts of hardships, they failed to locate the spot and returned. The Carbuncle was never afterward located, and, strange to say, it is no longer visible. Perhaps it is hidden with the other treasures of Mt. Washington under the care of the mountain spirits in the caverns and caves beyond the reach of human hand and sight.

Ellis River

During the early period in our history when hostility among the Indians toward the settlers became almost general, and the forages and surprises which warlike bands committed all along the coast filled the settlers with terror and alarm, there were many cruel and bloodthirsty deeds enacted in New England by the savages, and only behind the strongest barricade might any one feel safe. The actors in New England's war drama had changed; the scene of the show had shifted from the forest to the settlement. The redskins now occupied the center of the stage, and aghast the white settlers gazed on. Scant was the bounty now collected from the Solons of Massachusetts for Indian scalps. These pious legislators were watchful now in protecting their own.

Under cover of darkness, or from the dense ambush of the forest road, the swarthy messengers of death operated. Like avenging spirits, they swooped down when least expected, leaving behind a trail of death, devastation and blood; and, to add to the horror of it all, they employed the use of the cruel firebrand. Sometimes the bam and cattle of a white man were consumed in the stillness of the night. Then again, while wrapped in slumber, flames would burst forth from various parts of the house, and before aid could arrive both family and mansion would be in ashes; and often whole settlements in a single night were so completely enveloped in fire as to leave only charred and smoky ruins a few hours later.

It was at this epoch in New England's life that a band of marauding Indians from Canada, returning from a pillaging expedition along the coast, entered the settlement of Dover, N.H., and, rushing into the house of a white man who was absent from home, they seized the wife and before her very eyes murdered two of her children. The mother clasped the smallest child, an infant, in her arms, and she, together with her daughter, a beautiful young girl of eighteen, a small boy and a younger daughter were taken captives. Towards Canada the savages departed with their unhappy prisoners. Through thick forests, over high hills and steep mountain passes, wading

23

through swamps and marshes, fording rivers swollen with the rain, goaded by the taunts of their persecutors, these poor captives, the heartbroken mother, the frail and delicate young woman and the frightened children were hurried on.

At night their bed was the cold, hard earth. With scarcely any clothing, and famished from want of sufficient food, these brave women and children suffered unheard-of hardships. The mother, with her precious infant clasped closely to her breast, suffered without flinching. The sight of the reeking scalps of her murdered children, dangling at a warrior's belt, filled her heart with anguish and with woe; but, fearful for the living, she betrayed no sign of weakness.

At length, worn out and exhausted, both captors and captives stopped to rest on the banks of the Ellis River.

The chief, wearied of his charges, determined to kill them; but the cruel instincts of his savage heart must first be satisfied. He attempted to intimidate the faithful mother by pretending to strike the babe with his tomahawk; but the protecting arms of the brave mother shielded and encircled more closely the sleeping form. Then, as if by sudden impulse, he turned to the maiden and demanded of her a song. Whether it was the solitude of the peaceful wood and the laughing music of the rolling river that instilled into that uncivilized soul the desire for music, we know not; but in answer to his demand this beautiful young girl, gazing at her captor, sang in sorrowful, soul-stirring cadence, and through the forest the words of a hymn floated. Her beautiful eyes filled with tears, but unflinching she faced her tormentors. It was the music of a heart overburdened with sorrow, and at the first strains of her sad but melodious voice the eyes of these uncouth warriors dropped. When she had finished, the bloodiest one of the lot, he who had killed the children, stepped forward, tenderly took the baby from the mother's embrace and carried it, while the burdens of both women were lifted and the children were assisted on their way. The melody of this beautiful girl's voice had kindled a spark in these untutored beings, and the music had indeed charms to "soothe the savage breast."

J. S. English

The remainder of their journey to Canada was devoid of hardships. Everything which the Indians could do for their comfort was accomplished. They remained among the tribes of Canada for several months, but were treated with kindness and consideration, and were afterwards purchased and returned to their home by white settlers who had gone in search of them.

Ellis River and Jackson, N. H.

Once, there was a powerful tribe of Indians who inhabited a region close by the Ellis River, now known as Jackson, New Hampshire. The Sagamore had a beautiful daughter, the handsomest maiden of her race. So renowned was the beauty of this famous damsel, that braves from the tribes throughout New England and Canada and even from the distant and warlike Mohawks were among her suitors; but to all the maiden's answer was the same. Her father had determined that a brave of his own tribe, the most powerful among his young men, should be the husband of his daughter. The selection pleased the daughter but little for already she had listened with favor to the wooing of a noted warrior of a neighboring tribe.

Secretly the lovers met at night and renewed their vows of allegiance to one another, and at last, the young brave determined to press his suit with the Sagamore. Laden with presents of valuable furs and wampum, the ardent lover journeyed to the wigwam of the Sagamore. Earnestly he pleaded for the daughter of the Great Chief and at the feet of the Sagamore, as a token of his friendship, he laid his presents. The Sagamore listened intently to the warrior's love tale for he dared not openly refuse the representative of so powerful a tribe, but in his heart was disappointment and sadness, for he had reserved his daughter for the other. The old Sagamore called the chiefs of his tribe in council and all night they talked and deliberated. At length it was decided that both suitors should have equal favor and the most skilful archer should carry off the precious prize.

Accordingly, at a distance of fifty paces a round target was marked on a white birch tree, and each brave in turn was to display his skill with the bow. He of the distant tribe, strong and fearless, eyes blazing with excitement for the result, stepped forward – quickly he drew his bow, the whirring arrow sped straight to the birch, almost to the very center of the target. Victory shone on the bronze forehead, confidence beamed from his every feature as he strode toward the prize which awaited him. Then, forward came the sturdy form of one who towered above all the warriors of his race. His rank was high for the eagle plumes floated from his raven locks and the prowess of a chief marked his bearing. Deliberately he drew his bow and aimed. Snap! went the cord, and his winged messenger lodged in the very center of the target. A shout of triumph burst from the victorious tribe — while the calm and implacable warrior turned in the direction of the maiden. Short lived, however, was the shout of triumph; the impassive countenance had changed to a look of fierce rage. Instantly, the loser, seeing he had been vanquished, caught his sweetheart by the hand and speeding like the wind, they sought the wood. In swift pursuit followed the braves, the victorious archer foremost. Faster and nearer pressed the pursuers. The brave and his sweetheart, realizing that escape was impossible, made a desperate dash for the nearby river, reaching it but a few yards in advance of their pursuers. They hesitated for a moment only, and then both plunged headlong and were lost in the turbulent waters of Ellis Cascade.

Have you listened for the song of a siren, whose sweet strains rise above the roar of Ellis River? It is the lullaby of an Indian queen, softly crooning to her faithful lover.

Another story of Ellis River is that a beautiful Indian maiden admired and loved by all the young braves of her race, but so peerless in her beauty and accomplishments that no young man was deemed worthy of her—fled from the tribe.

Weeks and months were spent in search of her, but no trace could be found of the missing girl. One day, however, a party of Indians, returning from the hunt, saw a beautiful maiden and a young brave with long flowing hair like the girl's, which reached below his waist, seated on the banks of the river. They recognized the maiden as the beautiful girl who had disappeared. Her companion was a spirit or water nymph. Glancing up they perceived the war party, then both plunged into the river and disappeared. Ever afterward when the hunter reached Ellis River, he stopped at this point and sought the spirits to aid him in his quest, and, answering the prayer of the hunter, the water nymphs would call moose and deer and wild animals in great numbers from the woods.

Moosilauke and the Pemigewassets

Of the numerous peaks of the White Mountains range, none, not even Mount Washington, with its wealth of scenic splendor and legendary lore, from whose summit the Indians' great "Manitou" scattered his sunbeams and hurled his anger in thunderbolts, where now tourists gather to gaze in awe and wonderment upon the tumbled peaks and spurs of the mountains and the green swards of the valleys, surpasses in interest and beauty the bold pinnacle of old Moosilauke.

Situated some miles from its nearest neighbor, the Franconia Range, Moosilauke gazes with a sense of superiority at the others and looks toward Mount Washington with less reverence than disdain. Supreme ruler of his own domain, 4800 feet above the sea level, the highest elevation in New Hampshire east of Mount Lafayette, he seems conscious of fame in the possession of three distinct peaks.

The summit is a broad plateau of many acres with no big boulders such as characterize most of the White Mountains peaks. It is above the timber line, and Alpine plants and mountain cranberries constitute its only vegetation. On the north is a high, broad crest and further north is a blue dome,–Mount Blue. A long narrow ridge joins the north peak and the crest. The summit is the southern peak, and here is located the Tip Top House. On the east side of Moosilauke is the Jobildunk Ravine in the upper part of which is the Jobildunk Cascade. On the west slope is the head of an enormous slide over two thousand feet long, at an angle of about forty degrees and with a width varying from about fifteen to fifty feet. The most amazing of the natural wonders of Moosilauke is the vast Amphitheatrical Gulf, near the Benton Trail. It is eight hundred feet deep and a peculiar feature is that this great cavern is literally filled with growing trees whose verdure seems to suffer not at all from their strange location. The summit can be reached by three approaches—a carriage road from Warren, by a bridle path from Benton and by foot paths from North Woodstock and Warren Summit.

Indian Legends of the White Mountains

The view from the summit of Moosilauke cannot be surpassed by that from Mount Washington. Indeed, the isolation of this mountain from the other peaks gives it a decided advantage, and, unlike the higher mountains, there is never any fog or cloud envelopment to hinder the view. On one side the green fields of the bordering Connecticut Valley and the fertile farms of Vermont greet the vision, and in the distance the blue tops of the Adirondacks are plainly discernible. The peaks and ravines of New Hampshire and the valleys and meadow lands of the Granite State, blending with the pine forest of Maine, present a picture in which pastoral charms and rugged grandeur vie for ascendency. Toward the northeast, the beauty of the Franconia Mountains becomes doubly enhanced by nearby observance, while to the northwest is Mount Kinsman and in the rear, craning eagerly forward, the white head of Mount Cannon, both gazing in admiration on the tower of Moosilauke.

In the vicinity of Warren and Moosilauke lived the Pemigewasset Indians. The mountain received its name from the Indian words "Moosi" which means bald and "Auke," meaning place, and the "L" was afterwards inserted by the English for euphony. The Pemigewassets, a powerful tribe of the Nipmuck Nation, had all the popular superstitions of the New England Indians. In their minds the Great Spirit was wont to frequently visit the mountain top. The early harvest of the corn, the golden maize, the ripest fruit of the orchards, the fat carcass of the bear, moose or deer, the choicest of the hunter's quarry, all were offered in sacrifice to the Manitou at the foot of Moosilauke.

Well they understood the mood of the Manitou. When angry, the sky became clouded; Nepauz, the Divinity of the sun, hid his face; darkness enshrouded the mountain and the Manitou proclaimed his anger in the usual forms of lightning flashes and thunder. The wolf and bear roared and fought in the Jobildunk Ravine, and from the peak of Moosilauke the screams of the war eagle, Keneu, filled the valley below. When pleased, the mien of Moosilauke reflected the desires of the Manitou; Nepauz came forth in all his golden splendor, the salmon frolicked in the silver lake; the beavers became busy along the banks of the Connecticut; the denizens of the forests fled before the hunter's bow, and the squaws chatted and sang as they gathered the yellow maize.

The Pemigewassets belonged to the Algonquin race and were reckoned in their nation as a tribe of strength and power. The cruel Tarantines of the Provinces and the fierce "man eaters" or Mohawks, had measured the war-like propensities of this New Hampshire tribe and hesitated about engaging in war with the confederation to which they lent their aid. The name Pemigewasset was applied to this section of the mountain and from this the tribe received its name.

Passaconaway, the great Sagamore, for years ruled the Nipmuck Nation, a confederation which comprised the Nashuas, Souhegans, Amoskeags, Penacooks, Squamscotts and a half dozen other tribes, but at his death, dissatisfaction arose and internal warfare did much to weaken the strength of the league. The Pemigewassets still retained their prominence, however, and Wonalancet, son of Passaconaway, collected as best he could the scattered tribes of the Nipmucks. Following the advice of the illustrious Passaconaway, his son, Wonalancet made a covenant of peace with the English.

Philip of Mount Hope, known to the Indians as Pometacom, than whom no braver or more daring character is recorded in the annals of American history, determined to make a last attempt for the freedom of his race. With rare skill this natural leader had united the warring tribes; he impressed them with the idea that only in union remained their safety and preservation, and then with the sagacity of a military leader he planned for the complete destruction of the English. This courageous and tactful savage, endowed with the abilities which have written indelibly on the pages of American history the names of Washington, Grant, Sherman, Sheridan and a score of others, realized the immensity of his task and resources. He sought strength from far and near, and, had Wonalancet and other chiefs followed the example of the Colonists in the keeping of peace covenants, King Philip's War would occupy a different page in the history of New England.

Indian Legends of the White Mountains

Philip dispatched messengers to Wonalancet requesting his aid, but the Nipmuck warrior refused to violate his compact, consequently he incurred the displeasure of the warring tribes. Neither did he desire to join against his own race. Finding himself uncomfortably beset whichever way he turned, Wonalancet with his followers returned to the land of the Penacooks. The Colonists soon discovered him in his hiding place and being very eager to secure the aid on their own side of as many bloodthirsty savages as possible, dispatched a second deputation urging the chief to take sides with the English.

Wonalancet persistently and indignantly refused, and Captain Moseley, who had acquired considerable fame in previous Indian wars, was sent to disperse the Penacooks and Pemigewassets and to punish Wonalancet for his insubordination.

There was but one place of refuge for Wonalancet and, collecting his faithful followers, he fled to the mountain forests of New Hampshire. Here, among the thickets of the White Mountains, every foot of wilderness and every nook and cranny among the rocks and ledges of which were familiar ground, the Sachem of the Pemigewassets found safe shelter. Here, in the old home of his tribe he remained until the autumn when he was joined by Monocco or One-eyed John and Sagamore Sam, warriors who lately had engaged in many exciting adventures against the Colonists under the leadership of Philip.

In September, 1676, four hundred Indians had been enticed to come to Dover, under the pretense of a friendly conference with the English. Captain Waldron, with Hawthorne, Frost and Sill met the Indians with the English forces at Cocheco and planned a sham battle.

The Indians drew up in battle array on one side, the English on the other. The English so arranged it that by a clever coup they surrounded the red men and took them all captives. These who had engaged in Philip's War were hanged and quartered, Monocco and Sagamore Sam being among the number. The remainder, with the exception of a few, were sold into slavery. Wonalancet, with one hundred and fifty followers, a mere handful of his former strength, was allowed to depart. He fled to his former home; but at Penacook or Concord or even in the fastness of the mountains, there was no longer safety or happiness for Wonalancet, so on September 19, 1677, he journeyed to the St. Francis tribe in Canada and was never afterward heard from.

Cold Streams

A tale is told of an Indian brave famous among his tribe as a hunter and a warrior. He set out with a party of braves one day, hunting the moose. An immense animal larger than any moose which he had ever before beheld, appeared. The Indian fired at him and the arrow pierced the animal's shoulder, but the shot was not fatal and the moose enraged with pain crashed through the bushes. The Indian followed over stumps and logs, through briers and swamps. Tireless on the trail, the speediest of his tribe, he had far out-distanced his companions, who returned exhausted. For several days he continued the chase, but at last fell fatigued and dropped into a deep slumber. In his sleep, he dreamed of a vast hunting land, where game was plentiful, where the moose and deer and the bear roamed unmolested; where the lakes were alive with a horde of fluttering ducks; where the wild flowers filled the fields and the songs of the birds from the tree tops lulled the warriors to sleep; where the voice of the Great Spirit of Life was delivered from heaven, and where the braves lived only to war and to hunt.

In the midst of his dream, he was awakened by a loud voice, which commanded him to travel farther on. Opening his eyes, he beheld a Good Spirit who presented him with a flint-pointed spear with which he might capture the salmon, and a dry coal to kindle a fire and keep warm. He then continued his journey and by the shores of a lake halted and built his fire. Out of the fire a bursting flame leaped forth and there was a tremendous noise and explosion; a shower of rocks was thrown high in the air and clear and sparkling streams of water bubbled from the earth.

A cloud of smoke rolled up and dimmed the atmosphere, and in a voice of thunder the Great Spirit called, "Here the Great Spirit will dwell and will watch over and protect his children."

This spot serves as a perpetual reminder of the Manitou's prophecy, and the cold, clear water which spurted forth has been flowing since and is known to all visitors as "Cold Streams."

Rogers' Rangers and the Sack of St. Francis

In the village of St. Francis, Quebec, on the beautiful river which bears this name, lived the St. Francis tribe of Indians. In close alliance with the French Government, they were safe from the avenging muskets of the English settlers. At first their number was few, but under the protection of the French King, they soon gathered into the folds of the tribe, refugees from the Provincial Tarantines; the remnants of the once powerful Amariscoggins, the Pemigewassets and many others. Bound together by a common tie—hatred for the English—it is needless to say that hardly any venture of theirs which aimed at the destruction of the Colonists, was frustrated by the French.

And when one pictures these same savages under the guidance of their great Sachem, Passaconaway, members of a federation which feared not even the bloody Mohawks; and saw among the mountains the stately Pemigewassets enthusiastically pursuing the pleasures of the hunt, and the numerous canoes of the Amariscoggins floating over the lakes, engaged in spearing the salmon or daringly shooting the rapids; and compared this vision with conditions of the time, he observed a pitiful contrast. Obliged to battle against a distant invader, the red man had been driven back, back to the innermost haunts of the forest; forced to flee and hide at the white man's entrance; cruelly dispossessed of every article of value and no longer able to combat his foes, he was obliged to abandon forever the land of his birthright. Naturally, then, when the St. Francis braves went on the war path, it was with a feeling of exultation and satisfied revenge that they returned with English scalps. And yet, within their own domains, these Indians displayed but few of their savage propensities. A French missionary labored faithfully among them, and under his efforts they adopted the Christian religion. It has often been stated that his ardor was not, confined entirely to their spiritual welfare. However, be that as it may, while his patriotism may have overshadowed at times his religious zeal, it is certain that hatred of the English was so deeply rooted in the savage heart, that neither missionary nor governor could dissuade them; and impartial historians have justified the missionary by ascribing to him a character wholly devout and sincere in his purpose of saving souls; ready to lay down his life for his flock; intensely patriotic and true to his fatherland.

On the other hand, there was at this time, in New Hampshire, a body of as brave and daring men as ever lived; frontier fighters whose home was the forest and whose occupation was Indian fighting, "For King and Country," against an enemy whom they considered devoid of almost all the qualities of human beings. Against "savages, slightly in advance of the lower animals, with scarcely a redeeming virtue," Major Rogers with his band of sturdy New England frontiersmen, skilled in the art of woodcraft and with a thorough knowledge of Indian warfare, battled.

This famous guerilla company, composed of the picked men of the Colonists, had acquired a reputation far beyond the confines of New England; and "Rogers' Rangers" was a name coupled with the most daring adventures of travel and warfare.

On September 13, 1756, Sir Jeffrey Amherst summoned Major Rogers to his presence and the following conversation occurred: "Rogers, I am tired of the depredations made by that tribe of red devils on the St. Francis. They boast of six hundred white scalps hanging outside their tepees and are becoming bolder every day. We must teach them a lesson and likewise their French consorts. Prepare your men, Major, for a journey and wipe out every male inhabitant in the village—no quarter, mind you, but for the women and children! Remember, Rogers, spare only the women and children."

"As you command, General, I shall take ample revenge; and for once these redskins shall feel the strength of the Rangers. Good day, General," and turning on his heels the Major departed.

That same night Major Rogers at the head of his two hundred Rangers sallied forth, provisioned and prepared for a march through a hostile country so wild and repellant in parts as to discourage only the most hopeful. Through wild morasses and swamps; thickets so dense as to be almost impenetrable; over high rocky cliffs; through mountain passes; fording deep streams and rivers—nothing undaunted or dismayed, journeyed these hardy woodsmen. At length, after a march of twenty-two days they came within sight of the village.

It was about eight in the evening and a rest was ordered; sentinels were stationed and the men slept. Major Rogers with two privates went forward to reconnoiter.

He saw the tall spire of the church in the center of the village, then as he drew nearer, he perceived that a wedding was in progress; festivities were being indulged in—they were dancing and singing to the music of the Indian drums. The little church was in the center of the village and brilliantly lighted; the flickering candle flames illuminated the beautiful altar, to the right of which stood a solid silver image of the Blessed Virgin. On the walls were handsome paintings imported from France, and on the altar was a golden crucifix; without, the shouts and laughter of the Indians. Rogers watched the revelry throughout the night until early in the morning; and at two o'clock, when the noise had ceased, and, tired from their exertions the revelers were wrapped in slumber, he returned to the camp. The men were fast asleep. He dared not delay—this was his opportunity, and at 3.00 A.M. he aroused his men. He drew his command close to the village before he halted them. Then forming three divisions, they waited for the command of attack.

At the word they rushed forward; every man to his work. The Indians, surprised and startled, rushed hither and thither, but found no avenue of escape. Without any arms, they could offer no defense, and now began one of the bloodiest scenes of carnage which the world has ever witnessed. Some were struck down by their antagonists before they had a chance to cry out, others huddled together in their fright, were butchered like so many rats. Blood everywhere, and the sight of it enraged the Rangers. There was no distinction, men women and children were treated alike—"Kill and burn" was the cry! The faithful priest, true to his spiritual children and his faith rushed to the sanctuary of the altar for protection. With him went a group of a dozen or more Indians. The wedding party stoutly barricaded in their wigwam, were espied by two of the Rangers. Instantly the doors were battered down and Bradley and Farrington in a few short minutes had sent a dozen savages, men and women to eternity.

Heaps of dead bodies blocked the narrow streets of the village; blood flowed from every wigwam; the horrified screams of the wounded and those who had escaped the axe to suffer the dreadful penalty of fire, cooped up without any hope of escape, floated on the morning air. Wild with the sight of their butchery, a party of Rangers rushed to the chapel; the strong doors were like glass before the weighty axes of the woodsmen, but reaching within, a sight met their gaze which filled them with awe; they were arrested by the dazzling solemnity. There, on the altar with his hands folded on his breast, calmly stood the priest clad in his gorgeous vestments. Behind him were a dozen savages with faces lined with horror and despair. The eyes of the faithful missionary shone fearlessly. Like a Christian martyr of old, surrounded by the emblems of his sacred religion, in the glare of a hundred candle lights, a jeweled chalice at his right, and a golden crucifix on his left, ten thousand Rangers could not move to fear this valiant spirit.

"What seek ye, monsters?" cried he, in a voice which thrilled his every hearer. "Would ye carry your butchery to the house of God? Desist, devils, for this is the sanctuary of your Maker, and you are in the presence of Christ himself."

Inured as they were to cruelties and bloody deeds, hardened by their uncivilized associations, these wild creatures were indeed visibly affected. Not a man stirred, but ere many moments had passed, the golden vessels and the valuables in sight aroused their cupidity.

"We will give you quarter, Friar," cried one in authority. "Surrender now, surrender and you shall have quarter."

"Never!" cried the priest.

"A last time," called the voice, "surrender, or your blood be upon your own head!"

Reaching for the chalice the brave man elevated it in front of him, crying in a loud voice, "To your knees, monsters, to your knees."

This wonderful apparition had for a moment a marvelous effect. Some turned to flee, others obeying the command fell on their knees; but he who had spoken reached to his gun and fired. Tumbling to the foot of the altar with the sacred chalice clasped to his breast, the good priest fell dead. The Indians were dispatched in short order; the chalice wrested from the dead man's grasp and its sacred contents ruthlessly profaned; the golden crucifix and the silver statue and every article of value were appropriated. The torch was then applied, and in half an hour as the flames crept toward the steeple, the tower of the little church rocked and the chapel bell tolled its last sad mournful notes. In but a short time the whole village was in flames; the steeple crumpled and fell and the village of St. Francis with its inhabitants was no more. Three hours of the bloodiest carnage, the most atrocious cruelties and horrors ever executed upon a community by civilized beings, were occupied in the fulfilment of General Amherst's orders.

As the Rangers stood watching the progress of the fire, from the heap of the dead at the foot of the altar—according to legend—a voice arose which made the hearts of the Rangers jump. It said, "The Great Spirit of the Abenaquis will scatter darkness in the path of the accursed pale-faces! Hunger walks before and death strikes their trail! Manitou is angry when the dead speak. The dead have spoken!"

At seven o'clock in the morning not a single habitation remained. The Rangers had lost but one man and but six were wounded. Everything of value which could be carried with them had been plundered, and provisioning themselves for their return journey from a grain shed, they were ready for departure.

Rogers had fallen upon St. Francis and completed his work expeditiously; because he realized the fact that three hundred French and Indians were already on his trail and every day drawing nearer. Worn out and exhausted from their forced march of twenty-two days—obliged as they were again to face the forbidding forest with scarcely any rest, the lot of the Rangers was no easy one. The cool October blast chilled them to the marrow. Ignorant of the country, it was with difficulty that they made any progress at all. The French and Indians, well provisioned, were but a few miles in their rear, and so great was their confusion that for three days the Rangers wandered aimlessly in a dense swamp. On the fourth day they again struck the trail in the rear of their pursuers. They now decided upon a desperate measure of hope. The pangs of famine had already reached them; their provisions had been lost in the swamp and fearful of attracting the enemy by hunting for food, they were obliged to endure. It was determined to separate into nine parties and agreed that whatever body met the enemy, for the protection of their companions, would give battle. A short while after separation repeated firing proclaimed the fact that the enemy had been encountered by one party, and the sacrifice had been made; but too great was the sin of the Rangers to expect atonement at such a paltry price. The blood of three hundred men, women and children cried out for vengeance, and Rogers' Rangers were yet destined to pay the penalty for the sack of St. Francis. Ere the shores of Memphremagog were reached, famine had so reduced what remained of the band of two hundred that they were scarcely able to drag their emaciated forms along. Fearful of an ambuscade, they were ever on the watch for an unseen foe, and their moccasins and powder horns had long since been boiled to furnish sustenance.

Bradley, who had been foremost in the work of butchery, was the first to reach the Connecticut River at Upper Coos, eighteen days after his departure. From here he lost his course and wandered over the mountains, seeking shelter in a cave where a year afterwards his parched bones and skull were found by a party of hunters and, scattered about, silver brooches and wampum plunder from St. Francis.

General Amherst had dispatched Lieutenant Stevens with provisions to meet the stragglers, but he had missed them and returned. The commands under Lieutenant Philips and Sergeant Evans suffered horribly. Day after day with throats parched from lack of water, not a morsel of food passing their lips, the men under Lieutenant Philips plodded on. He saw them one by one drop by the wayside, some too weak to utter even a cry; others with glassy eyes bulging from their sockets, and skin so drawn and parched as to be almost transparent; in their delirium, uttering agonizing cries and bitter imprecations, and haunted by the curses of the dying victims of St. Francis, they would shriek and start at the imaginable advent of a foe.

At last ready to sink from hunger they determined to kill an Indian prisoner and feast on human flesh and blood, but it happened that on that very day a muskrat was killed, and the Indian's life was spared. Still more terrible were the sufferings of Sergeant Evans' men. Their only nourishment for days and weeks was birch bark and roots. Delirious in their suffering, they came upon the dead bodies of their late companions. They sat down to a feast of human flesh. Like ravenous beasts they tore the flesh from the bones, built a fire, and when they had gorged themselves on this human diet, filled their knapsacks with steaks cut from the dead bodies.

Lieutenant George Campbell in command of another party, was four days without food of any kind when they discovered three human bodies floating down the river. The bodies were scalped and horribly mutilated, yet the famished Rangers pounced upon them like so many wolves, and, not even waiting to build a fire, devoured the raw flesh.

Major Rogers, who had throughout his trying march never lost his wonderful nerve, also reached this section. He collected the Rangers who had safely arrived thus far and alone started down the river in search of assistance. He constructed a crude raft, floated down the river, and, after a hazardous journey, procured help. Canoes were built, and in ten days, true to his pledge, Major Rogers returned with the promised succor to his surviving Rangers.

The people of Coos found many relics and eloquent signs of this ill-fated expedition, and to this day tell tales which have been transmitted from Indians. They firmly believed in the prophetic curses which followed the sacrilege at the chapel and the pillaging of the silver statue and the sacred vessels.

On the Connecticut River near the head of the Fifteen Miles Falls, a party of nine Rangers secured the services of an Indian guide who agreed to conduct them through the "Great Pass" (the Notch) of the mountains to the settlement. This party had the silver image, weighing eight pounds, stolen from the church. The guide led them to Israel's River in Jefferson, N.H., through the pathless forests along the shores of the stream to the deep, snow-laden gorges at the foot of the White Hills. Pretending to fear the wrath of the Manitou if he dared enter the forests of the sacred Agiochook, the Indian made a rude birch-bark map and gave it to one of the Rangers, at the same time apparently accidently scratching his hand with the poisonous fangs of a rattlesnake. Plodding with desperate efforts through the deep snow, braving as best they could the cold storm, they continued their journey but a short way when the poison of the rattlesnake did its work. The Ranger became mad and in the violence of his delirium he rushed to the top of a high precipice and flung himself into the depths below. The survivors, weak from their long and perilous march, with scarcely sufficient strength to carry themselves, concluded to bury their plunder in a cave on the mountain, where the superstitious horror of the Indian would prevent his entering, thus protecting their treasure and their lives.

Deceived by the false chart of their treacherous guide, they wandered in a circle for several days, suffering extreme cold and hunger. One by one they succumbed to the fatigue and cold. Several years afterwards some hunters found a barkless spot on a pine tree at the entrance to a wild ravine on which were many partially obliterated characters engraved by some rude tool. Near this were some rusty buttons, decayed cloth, a small copper kettle and the metallic parts of a gun. At the foot of a steep bank, six rusty gun barrels were found and what resembled the relics of a pile of knapsacks. An old hunter, exploring for this hidden treasure, sought shelter from a terrible storm in a cave, where in the farthest corner he discovered several stones forming a pile. Beneath was found a hatchet heavily incrusted with rust, also a roll of birch bark covered with the wax of wild bees. In the roll was found an Indian-tanned fawn skin on which were many mysterious hieroglyphics.

In 1815, the golden candlesticks were found near Lake Memphremagog, but no trace has ever been heard of the silver statue. Once, however, a number of years ago a lonely hunter wandered far into the mountains and when nightfall came, he was close to the summit of Mt. Adams. During the night a terrific storm arose; thick black clouds rolled over the mountains, the lightning flashed, thunder boomed and the wind raged and howled in a terrible manner.

The clouds broke, and there suspended over a deep chasm was the skeleton form of an Indian. Then the voice of the storm ceased, and from the deep abyss below came the screams of lost spirits; the mountain mist rolled back, the voices stopped and supreme quietness reigned, while before the astonished vision of the hunter appeared a great stone church. Within the church was an altar brilliantly lighted; the glow from the candles illumined the whole interior—the golden candlesticks, crucifixes and statues on the altar dazzled in their splendor, and from a sparkling censer rose curling wreaths of incense. Around the altar appeared a tribe of savages kneeling in profound silence; then the church spire, church and altar vanished, and down the steep mountain trailed the long line of savages in solemn silence. Before all, as if borne by some heavenly spirit, floated the glittering statue of silver, which, as it penetrated into the deep shadows, changed into the form of the St. Francis Friar; then, sparkling again, the image of the Blessed Virgin shone for a moment and disappeared in the side of a mountain ledge.

Such is the story of St. Francis, the sack and the massacre, and the hardships of the return journey by Rogers' Rangers being a true narrative of one of the bloodiest events ever perpetrated by civilized beings on their fellowmen. The prophecy and unnatural happenings are but legendary accounts handed down by settlers and savages.

Legend of Eagle Mountain

Between Ellis River and Wild Cat Brook, one of the most dashing and beautiful of the mountain streams, lie the Eagle Mountains, a low range, in places very craggy and rocky, named from the eagles who inhabited the upper cliffs in large numbers.

Early in the seventeenth century, when the colony of Massachusetts Puritans, frantic in their religious zeal were industriously engaged cutting the ears off peaceful Quakers and banishing from the colony all who dared to worship God in a manner contrary to their commands, there lived among them, one, Thomas Crage, a man of sound common sense and good Christian ideals. Very happy in his new home with his young wife and child of six, he cared little for the religious turmoil within the colony. Being a man of very honest and independent nature, he naturally rebuked all attempts whatsoever at interference with his personal affairs. His wife was a young and handsome woman, devotedly attached to her husband and child. She cared little for the gossips of the town and found plenty to keep her mind occupied in attending to her own affairs. However, this happy family was not to pass unmolested. Minding one's own business in those days was considered a suspicious trait, and the beauty of the young wife had already attracted attention. Surely no woman could possess such comely features unless bewitched by the evil spirit! The gossips gadded and observed as they went from house to house; the learned minister and the town authorities talked the matter over, and dark hints were thrown out about Mistress Crage and her husband. The doughty little Pilgrim disdained to notice their slander, and the stalwart husband would have laid low the person who dared to refer to these dark reproaches in his presence.

The wicked, slanderous tongues of these religious rattlesnakes were fast doing their work. The poison had been carefully- spread, and these pious God-fearing wretches who had fled from a cruel motherland because of its religious persecutions, were about to stain the shores of this new found Paradise with the blood of an innocent woman.

Indian Legends of the White Mountains

The redskins of the forest sometimes in their savage and barbarous customs propitiated their Great Manitou with a human sacrifice. Their white brethren, civilized and cultured, who appeared shocked at the horrid atrocities of the Indians, to do justice to a merciful God who had guided them thither, cut off the ears and noses of unbelievers and branded them with red hot irons; and, lastly, when their piety had reached its highest culmination, they, too, offered human sacrifices in propitiation.

Such was the period of New England's real reign of terror, when the beautiful and unfortunate Mrs. Crage chanced to live.

Fortunate indeed was the person who happened to escape the clutches of the Puritanical law. Pleasures were proscribed, not because of any evil or unholy result which would follow, but simply and solely because of the enjoyment afforded. Mrs. Crage was condemned as a witch because of her beauty. Despite the protests and pleadings of her husband, she was hanged as a witch.

Morose and sorrowful over the death of his wife, Thomas Crage lived now only for his child. He seldom spoke with his neighbors, and at night after his labors in the field were finished he would coddle and play with her.

One day while at work clearing his land, he was startled to hear cries from the child whom he had left in the house. He hurried home and rushing into the room where she had been accustomed to play, found it was vacant. Hastily scanning the surroundings he readily understood what had transpired. His child was gone; Indians had been there and had taken her away.

With one thought only, he followed in pursuit day and night with scarcely any food or rest; but no trace could he find of the Indians.

Wearied and exhausted, he arrived among the Pequawket Indians in the White Mountains. Diligently he searched their tribes and anxiously inquired for the missing babe, but to no avail, and not knowing whither to proceed, he rested here.

On the southern slope of Eagle Mountain in a deep cavern he built a cabin. Strong and healthy, he hunted and trapped, living by the fruit of his own endeavors. He was admired by the Indians, who first had feared the silent man but afterward learned to love him. Although his heart was filled with sorrow, he did not lose hope—he rather divined that one day he would find his daughter, and he believed that the Indians had stolen her not from any motive of malice or revenge, but to give to some squaw as was their custom, who had lately lost her own papoose. He was eagerly sought by the Indians for his skill in sickness. His long years of solitude had taught him the use of the various herbs and their curative and healing powers. Always welcome, yet seldom speaking, he was a frequent visitor at the Indians' camp fires.

It happened one day that an Androscoggin from that tribe in Maine journeyed hither. He climbed the cliffs in search of eagle feathers with which he might decorate his chief on his return; but losing his footing, he fell and was dashed among the rocks. Miraculously, he was not killed and the lone hunter came to his aid. He carried the Indian to his cabin; there mixed herbs for a liniment, dressed his bruises, reset the broken bones and in a month mused the Indian back to health. Departing, the red man was filled with gratitude toward the hunter. From him he heard of the fruitless quest for his missing daughter who had been stolen twenty years before. The savage determined to aid his "pale-face" friend. Prudence was the name of the girl, and with this name on his lip, the Indian strode forth.

Toward Canada he traveled, and in a few days he reached the domain of the St. Francis Indians. From wigwam to wigwam he journeyed until he reached the tepee of the chief, an aged warrior, whose furrowed and wrinkled visage and snow-white locks plainly told the trials and tribulations of a century of years. At the door of his tepee was a beautiful maiden who was directing a band of young warriors just returned from the hunt. Queen of the tribe, the daughter of the old chief, she was a true Indian princess. Her voice, her look, her action, her whole manner, portrayed the dignity of a ruler—one accustomed to command and be obeyed.

The Androscoggin, in respectful manner halted before this beautiful Amazon and carefully scrutinizing her handsome countenance, in the low guttural tone of the Indian, speaking in broken English, murmured the word "Prudence." Eagerly the Androscoggin watched the effect upon her. For an instant, a perplexed look stole over the girl's countenance but it immediately changed into a gaze of wonder and amazement. Her eyes flashed eagerly and curiously and in the St. Francis tongue she demanded where he had heard the name before. For years she had cherished this familiar name in her memory, not knowing whence it had come, having only a faint recognition of its connection with her childhood days. The Androscoggin asked her to bring forth the chief, and then seating himself beside the old Sagamore he related the tale told him by the hermit.

The eyes of the maiden blazed with excitement as he proceeded and when he related the trials of the father they filled with tears. The old chief nodded his assent when the brave had finished and pronounced her name Prudence. Under the Indian exterior and manner was hidden the soul of a white woman and she said to the Androscoggin warrior: "Go forth, and may the Manitou guide thee! Bring back to the wigwam of Chikonimee, the great white warrior who is my father! Tell him that the Indians love the father of Amateka and he will be the chief of all the St. Francis tribe!"

The Androscoggin returned to Eagle Mountain and, finding the lone hunter, related to him his discovery. The old man was overjoyed to hear from his daughter. He bade good-bye to the Pequawkets and with four of their warriors furnished him as body-guard, proceeded to the St. Francis Indians. Overcome at the sight of his daughter the old man fell on his knees and thanked the chief for protecting her during all these years. The heart of the daughter responded to the white man's call; fondly she embraced the old man and proclaimed him "Chief of the Indians of the St. Francis." From long years in the forests, he had become familiar with the various Indian tongues and customs and indeed looked upon the red men as his friends and brothers.

He was hailed as the great war chief of the St. Francis, and years afterwards when the Indians of Massachusetts sought help against the white invaders, the "Great White Chief" thirsting for revenge, with his faithful band swooped down upon the settlement formerly his home; and dealt a crushing defeat to the white settlers who thirty years before had hanged a pretty young pilgrim wife on the charge of witchcraft.

Captain Lovewell's Fight with Paugus

On the borderland of what are now the States of Maine and New Hampshire, in the valley of the Saco, lived the Pequawket Indians. Fryeburg was the center of their village, and during the troublesome period when incursions on the white settlers and Indian massacres were disturbing the quietude of this peaceful region, Paugus was chief of the Pequawkets.

On the frontier, the mere mention of this name was sufficient to strike terror into the stoutest heart. He was a giant in stature, and over his massive shoulders, he wore a huge bear skin. Time and again did the Pequawket warriors swoop down upon the settlers, ruthlessly scalping, burning and destroying. Foremost in every battle was the immense form of Paugus, striking with his great stone battle-axe right and left. He wielded this huge weapon with a certainty of death, and although he had been shot at and encountered face to face the bravest of the English in deadly combat, he always escaped unharmed. Many believed him to bear a charmed life, and this belief coupled with his gigantic strength and fierce courage made the Pequawket chief the dread of the frontier.

> "'Twas Paugus led the Pequ'k't tribe;
> As runs the fox, would Paugus run;
> As howls the wild wolf would he howl;
> A huge bear skin had Paugus on."

When the guns of the settlers and Indians were quiet, Paugus would journey to the mountains to hunt. His remarkable strength enabled him to beard Bruin in the fastness of the mountain caves, and single handed with his mighty battle-axe, he would slay both bear and moose. Skilled in the tactics of the Indian warfare, he was wary and cautious, always prepared for surprises and ready for defense. He would assemble his war canoes on the waters of Saco pondand from his high seat on an immense boulder called "Jockey Cap" observe the antics of his warriors. "Jockey Cap" is a monstrous boulder, one of the largest in this section, and a natural cavity in the rock forms a perfect seat which allows the observer to overlook the entire pond, while he himself remains unseen.

Such were conditions along the border, when Captain Lovewell with a party of thirty-five set out in search of Paugus and his warriors. They departed from Ossipee, after building a fort and leaving reinforcements to be called on in case of necessity. They were further stimulated by the reward of one hundred pounds offered for each Indian scalp by the Massachusetts General Court.

On the 7th of May, Lovewell and his party arrived in the vicinity of Saco pond, expecting to encounter the Indians. A report of a gun was the only trace of the enemy and they proceeded in the direction of the sound. On the following day, May the 8th, an Indian with two fowl in his hand was seen. The English fired on him but failing to hit him, the Indian, taking careful aim, returned the fire and mortally wounded Captain Lovewell. Ensign Wyman, who was immediately behind the captain, raised his piece to his shoulder, and after deliberate aim, sent a bullet through the savage's heart. The devout chaplain, with a prayer on his lips, rushed forward and insured his one hundred pounds revenue by scalping the Indian. Having left their packs behind on the previous day, they now hurried back, but the wily Paugus had been there ahead of them. He had carefully counted the packs, and, expecting their return, secreted his men in ambush and patiently awaited.

The English returned and when all were centered around the packs the Pequawket chief gave the signal, instantly the Indians arose, surrounding the English on all sides, the mighty Paugus in the lead. Paugus was well known to many of the settlers and his presence in battle ordinarily, was sufficient to instill despair in the ranks of the English; but the encounters of Lovewell had not been without hardship, and it was with a determination to do or die, that this little band took their stand. The Indians at the first charge fired a volley over the heads of their antagonists and requested them to surrender, thinking, no doubt, that they would not dare resist since Paugus had behind at least seventy-five men. This failed to impress the English, however, and the brave Lovewell, although mortally wounded, still led his forces and answered, "Only at the muzzles of your guns will we surrender." They then rushed forward, forcing the Indians to retreat several rods, and firing a volley which killed many among them. Paugus soon gathered his forces though and in turn pressed the English who left behind nine dead and three wounded. It was in this retreat that the brave captain fell, unable longer to survive his wounds.

All day the fight continued, waxing fierce on both sides. Above the din of battle could be heard the howls of the Indians and screams and curses of the dying and occasionally the hurrah and cheers of the English, betokening a favorable change in the battle.

In the midst of the fight, Solomon Keyes on the English side, was wounded three times, and fearing lest he would be left on the battlefield and fall a victim to the atrocious cruelties vented upon the Indian captives, he crawled toward the pond. There, perceiving a canoe, he managed to scramble into it and in the bottom of the boat fell unconscious. By the graces of a friendly current, the canoe drifted close to the fort of Ossipee, where he mustered sufficient strength to call for help. His friends at the fort answered his cries and came to his rescue.

During the heat of the battle, the savages wrought to a point of frenzy, were powwowing and howling in their war dance, when Ensign Wyman crept stealthily toward them and shot the leader, who proved to be Wahowa, a famous chief, second in command only to Paugus. This affair has been graphically if homely described in the verse:

"Good Heavens I they dance the pow-wow dance,
    What horrid yells the forest filled!
    The grim bear couches in his den,
    The eagle seeks the distant hill.
"'What means this dance, this pow-wow dance?'
    Stern Wyman said; with wondrous art,
    He crept full near, his rifle aimed,

Indian Legends of the White Mountains

And shot the leader through the heart."

Along about evening Paugus and John Chamberlain both happened to go down to the pond at the same time, to wash out their guns which had become heated from constant firing. They recognized each other and both agreed after washing their guns to commence loading at the same moment. Paugus in loading secured an advantage, as his bullet was of such a size it rolled easily down the barrel. While Chamberlain was using his ramrod, Paugus brought up his gun to prime, and realizing his advantage, said, "Paugus, the great chief of the Pequawkets will kill the pale-face warrior. No more the white man will gather scalps among the Pequawkets." Chamberlain finished his loading and struck the breech of his gun on the ground. Like a flash he then brought his weapon to his shoulder and fired. The bullet pierced the heart of Paugus and the brave chief fell dead at the white man's feet without uttering a cry. Chamberlain's gun from long use had become so worn that it primed itself; this fact saved his life.

Towards midnight the battle ceased, the remaining English retreated and fourteen eventually reached the fort. The Indians lost many more; and some weeks afterwards a party of English returned and found Captain Lovewell, whom they buried. The death of Paugus disheartened the Pequawkets and henceforth the valley of the Saco became quiet. The Pequawkets retired to the headwaters of the Connecticut, joined the Amariscoggins and subsequently became absorbed by the St. Francis tribe.

In commemoration of this fight, the colonists changed the name of the pond from Saco to Lovewells, and the memory of the men who gave up their lives in this wilderness is preserved by a tablet containing their names, which has been placed on the battleground.

www.ingramcontent.com/pod-product-compliance
Lightning Source LLC
Chambersburg PA
CBHW022133280326
41933CB00007B/674